TO:

_____

_____

FROM:

_____

_____

Thoughts and Reflections on Billy Graham's Life Principles
Copyright © 2005 by The Zondervan Corporation
ISBN-10: 0-310-81060-4
ISBN-13: 978-0-310-81060-5

Unless otherwise noted, all quotations and photographs are used by permission of the Billy Graham Evangelistic Association, 1 Billy Graham Parkway, Charlotte, NC 28201.

Photograph on pp. 51-52 reproduced by permission from InterVarsity Christian Fellowship/USA, PO Box 7895, Madison, WI 53707-7895.

Photograph on pp. 14-15 reproduced by permission from Youth for Christ, PO Box 4478, Englewood, CO 80155.

Painting on pp. 52-53 reproduced by permission from Campus Crusade for Christ, 100 Lake Hart Drive, Orlando, FL 32832.

Quotation on p. 125 from the closing session of the ECPA Publishing University, Bloomingdale, IL, November 9, 2004.

Special thanks is given to the Archives of the Billy Graham Center, Wheaton College, Wheaton, IL.

Associate Publisher: Tom Dean
Compiler: *The Livingstone Corporation.* Project staff include: Andy Culbertson, Jennifer Karrer, Kirk Luttrell, Christopher D. Hudson, Mary Horner Collins.
Design Manager: Kathy Needham
Production Management: Bev Stout
Cover and interior design: Kirk Luttrell, *The Livingstone Corporation*

Printed in the United States of America

05 06 07 / WPW / 5 4 3 2 1

COMMEMORATIVE 2005 CRUSADE EDITION

THOUGHTS & REFLECTIONS ON
BILLY GRAHAM'S
Life Principles

inspirio™

INTRODUCTION

As Billy Graham brings his crusade to New York City in June 2005, what a fitting time to reflect on and honor his life and work.

As a teenage farm boy from Charlotte, North Carolina, young Billy responded to God's calling on his life. The ministry that resulted from that calling has been nothing short of remarkable. He has faithfully extended the invitation to follow Jesus Christ to men and women of all races, backgrounds, and cultures, impacting thousands of lives around the globe. While many evangelists have had far-reaching ministries, few have had the international renown of Dr. Graham, and fewer still have maintained the level of integrity that has characterized the Billy Graham Association for over half a century.

Billy Graham has built his life upon solid biblical principles, and his ministry continues to stand firm on that foundation. His love for God and his Word, and a commitment to the simplicity of the gospel message have served as the structure supporting every aspect of his evangelistic outreach. Within the pages of this book you will hear from family members, friends, and acquaintances describing the values that have characterized Billy Graham's life and ministry. You will take a pictorial tour through some of the Billy Graham Crusades, and you will read Dr. Graham's own reflections about his faith and vision.

We hope you gain new insights into the man, Billy Graham. And beyond that, we hope this book will encourage new faith and commitment to the God he so faithfully serves.

Voices You'll Hear

The people you will meet in these pages are a few of the many who have walked with Billy Graham throughout his life and ministry. Some of them are family; some have supported him; some have served alongside him.

BUSBY, RUSSELL—BGEA photographer.

CROWLEY, MARY—BGEA board member; friend of Billy Graham.

FERM, ROBERT O.—BGEA Team member.

FORD, LEIGHTON—BGEA Associate Evangelist; Billy Graham's brother-in-law.

GRAHAM, MELVIN THOMAS—Billy Graham's brother.

GRAHAM, MORROW COFFEY—Billy Graham's mother.

GUSTAFSON, ROY W.—Evangelist and college friend of Billy Graham; BGEA Associate Evangelist.

JENKINS, JERRY—Bestselling author; consultant and contributing editor for *Just As I Am*

LANDES, JAMES H. (DR.)—Executive Secretary of Executive Board, Baptist General Convention of Texas, Dallas; long-time friend of Billy Graham.

MCELROY, CATHERINE G.—Billy Graham's sister.

POLLOCK, JOHN CHARLES (REV., DR.)—Billy Graham's biographer.

SHEA, GEORGE BEVERLY—Radio broadcaster, 1929-52; BGEA "charter member"; soloist at BGEA crusades.

SMITH, OSWALD J.—Founder, The People's Church, Toronto; active in Billy Graham's ministry.

VAN KAMPEN, ROBERT C.—Personal friend of Billy Graham; member of BGEA Board of Directors.

WILSON, GRADY—BGEA Team member, 1947-present; boyhood friend of Billy Graham.

Table of Contents

Life Principle 1

Go Into All the World and Preach the
Good News *(Mark 16:15)* 8

Life Principle 2

I Have Become All Things to All Men *(1 Cor. 9:22)* 16

Life Principle 3

I Am Not Ashamed of the Gospel *(Rom. 1:16)* 26

Life Principle 4

Seek First His Kingdom and His
Righteousness *(Matt. 6:33)* 34

Life Principle 5

In Humility Consider Others Better
than Yourselves *(Phil. 2:3)* 42

Life Principle 6

A Cheerful Look Brings Joy to the Heart *(Prov. 15:30)* 52

Life Principle 7

Listen to His Voice *(Deut. 30:20)* 58

Life Principle 8

He Must Become Greater; I Must
Become Less *(John 3:30)* 66

Life Principle 9

Do Not Swerve to the Right or the Left *(Prov. 4:27)* 74

Life Principle 10

He Delights in Men Who Are Truthful *(Prov. 12:22)* 86

Life Principle 11

Apart From Me You Can Do Nothing *(John 15:5)* 94

Life Principle 12

Work Together for the Truth *(3 John 1:8)* 100

Life Principle 13

Whatever You Do, Work at It With All
Your Heart *(Col. 3:23)* 106

Life Principle 14

Be ... Not Greedy for Money, but Eager to Serve *(1 Peter 5:2)* 112

Life Principle 15

Pray Continually *(1 Thess. 5:17)* 120

Urbana Student Missionary
Convention, 1976

— Life Principle 1 —

GO INTO ALL *the* WORLD *and* PREACH *the* GOOD NEWS

Jesus' command to spread the Gospel message has been the foundation of the worldwide evangelistic ministry of Billy Graham.

There are many types of evangelism as [Billy] has said. If you could sit down and talk to a person a year or two after they had come forward at a Crusade, you would discover that often that was the moment something had happened inside their heart and then they walked forward physically. But many steps had led up to this decision. I feel all of this is evangelism and the Crusade is simply one segment. Billy does not limit his evangelism to one particular ministry.

RUSS BUSBY

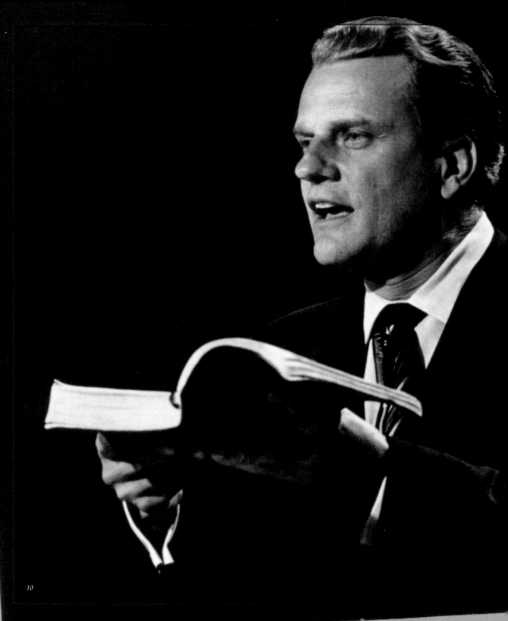

Go Into All *the* World *and* Preach *the* Good News

One of the most impressive places he has spoken was the Waldorf Astoria Hotel in New York to a Jewish organization. He started by saying that he would be betraying his cause if he spoke about anything other than what he believed. . . . But Billy . . . used [only] illustration[s] from the Old Testament. He finished with simply saying, "that really the only difference in what you believe and what I believe is that I believe that Jesus was the Messiah and you are still looking for the Messiah." . . . I feel his honesty is why he is invited back to many places and because he is not offensive, yet he has never failed to present Christ clearly.

Russ Busby

Crusade, 1968

GO INTO ALL *the* WORLD *and* PREACH *the* GOOD NEWS

In Paraguay during the South American tour . . . [Billy] went in to visit President Stroessner. This was a military state. He talked about many things. I was there, took a few pictures, and stood off to the side. . . . He spoke about many things and then just before he left, (he sensed it was about time to leave), he said, "Mr. President, I would like to tell you what happened to me when I was a young college student." And he gave a very simple, beautiful, to-the-point testimony of how he had accepted Christ, believed the Bible, and it had changed his entire life.

RUSS BUSBY

Congress on Evangelism,
Berlin, Germany, 1966

14

Go Into All *the* World *and* Preach *the* Good News

In my opening address I reminded the delegates [who had attended] the 1910 Edinburgh conference, "One of the purposes of this World Congress on Evangelism is to make an urgent appeal to the world church to return to the dynamic zeal for world evangelization that characterized Edinburgh fifty-six years ago. . . . The evangelistic harvest is always urgent. The destiny of men and of nations is always being decided. Every generation is crucial; every generation is strategic. But we are not responsible for the past generation, and we cannot bear full responsibility for the next one. However, we do have *our* generation! God will hold us responsible at the Judgment Seat of Christ for how well we fulfilled our responsibilities and took advantage of our opportunities."

BILLY GRAHAM, *Just As I Am*

— *Life Principle 2* —

I HAVE BECOME ALL THINGS *to* ALL MEN

Throughout his life Billy Graham has followed the example of the apostle Paul, who made himself accessible to people from every walk of life in order to reach them with the message of Christ.

❊❊❊❊❊❊❊❊❊❊❊❊❊❊❊❊

Billy is as far as he can be, I think, truthful, sincere, a proclaimer of the Word of God, who has been graced with looks and size and all of those qualities that go into charisma, plus a gift from God that allows him to speak to kings and to princes and to the ordinary man in a very effective way.

JAMES H. LANDES

With President Kim Il Sung,
North Korea, 1992

I Have Become All Things *to* All Men

I'm sure [Billy] could use words that I wouldn't understand if he wanted to. But if I couldn't understand them, then ninety percent of the public wouldn't either. So he has been very clear, very plain and very simple in his ministry. He has brought people to the Lord that I sincerely believe would never have come to the Lord had he tried to show his education and his intellectual ability.

MELVIN THOMAS GRAHAM

Oakland A's, 1971

I Have Become All Things *to* All Men

I think each person in each movement ha[s] certain people that they are unable to reach. For a middle-class American from his background, the fact that Billy has been able to reach people from the very, very wealthy to the very poor is an indication first of how universal the Gospel is, and second, how God can take us from our backgrounds and widen our abilities and our ministry.

Leighton Ford

With earthquake victims, Guatemala, 1976

I Have Become All
Things *to* All Men

He practices to retain a simplicity in his preaching and I have always listened to him in real amazement at the remarkably clear way he can express certain heavy theological concepts and make it sound almost like kitchen conversation. Yet he has said in words that a twelve-year-old child would understand some concepts that advanced theologians struggle with.

ROBERT O. FERM

I HAVE BECOME ALL
THINGS *to* ALL MEN

The *message* of the Gospel never changes—and for good reason: God never changes, and neither does our basic spiritual need nor His answer to that need. But the *methods* of presenting that message do change—and in fact they must change if we are to keep pace with a changing world. If we fail to bridge the gap between us and those we hope to reach, our message will not be communicated, and our efforts will be in vain. During this century, God has given us new tools to do His work—electronic and visual tools, such as radio, films, television, telephones—and each of these has played an important role in the expansion of our ministry.

BILLY GRAHAM, *Just As I Am*

Johnny Carson, 1972

Preaching early in his ministry

— *Life Principle 3* —

I Am Not Ashamed *of the* Gospel

Billy Graham's message has never faltered; he has been true to the Gospel of Christ from the beginning of his ministry to the present day.

[Billy] goes about doing good. We have men who have unusual gifts of mind, but when you consider Billy, he stands apart, because he's an international figure who has remained true to the Gospel, who has stood in the courts of the great universities. And after standing there, though there were those who still differed with him, he leaves as a rule with the great majority of them at least respecting him.

James H. Landes

I Am Not Ashamed
of the Gospel

I must say in . . . oral presentation that Billy stayed clean and pure, and I have heard him speak to the heads of nations, to the ambassadors, to all of the ranks, politically, of the whole world. I have never seen him vary his message. I have great affection for him, because I think somehow he has a gift from God to say the right thing at the right time, but never to compromise in any way. I think it's a gift of the Spirit. I really do. I have just been moved over and over.

JAMES H. LANDES

I Am Not Ashamed
of the Gospel

He has grown tremendously . . . in the way
he speaks and his delivery and in experience, intelligence, and knowledge. . . . [But]
there's no change in his message whatever.
The message is still the same sound evan-
gelical message that he has always preached
and is preaching as strong today than ever
before.

Oswald J. Smith

Reading at home, 1972

Trafalgar Square, London, 1954

I Am Not Ashamed
of the Gospel

I recall an old Methodist preacher who came to Harringay Arena in London in 1954. "I have come here every night for ninety-three nights," he told us, "and I have heard only one message." He meant it as a compliment, for he knew as I did that there *is* only one Christian message.

BILLY GRAHAM, *Just As I Am*

Life Principle 4

SEEK FIRST HIS KINGDOM *and* HIS RIGHTEOUSNESS

Billy Graham is characterized by clear priorities—his primary allegiance has always been to the calling God has on his life.

My exhaustion was caused not just by the intensive schedule. A doctor who was also an evangelist once told me that the hardest work a person can do is preach an evangelistic sermon. Whether that is true or not, I don't know. What I do know is that evangelistic preaching is physically and emotionally draining. One reason it is draining for me is that I am constantly driving for commitment. Another reason is that speaking of matters with eternal consequences is a great responsibility, and I am always afraid I won't make the message clear or will say something that is misleading.

BILLY GRAHAM, *Just As I Am*

SEEK FIRST HIS KINGDOM *and* HIS RIGHTEOUSNESS

Overseas, there are many people that have not heard of Billy Graham . . . depending upon what country of the world you are in. When you get to the heads of state, most of them definitely know about Mr. Graham. They maybe don't know a whole lot but they have respect for him. In the cases I'm familiar with, they have very openly received him not as a preacher, but they have received him really as an ambassador from the U.S. knowing that he was respected here. . . . But they were not aware that he was really an ambassador, as he has said many times, . . . representing heaven and not the U.S.

RUSS BUSBY

President Boris Yeltsin, Moscow, 1991

SEEK FIRST HIS KINGDOM *and* HIS RIGHTEOUSNESS

❉❉❉❉❉❉❉❉❉❉❉❉❉❉

Billy has stuck to evangelism. He hasn't become President of the United States of America and he hasn't tried to. And yet he could have become President in all probability but Billy has turned down every offer of every kind and has stuck strictly to evangelism. He still remains primarily an evangelist. That's what he is. And he's doing a work the likes of which no other evangelist has ever done in the history of the world.

OSWALD J. SMITH

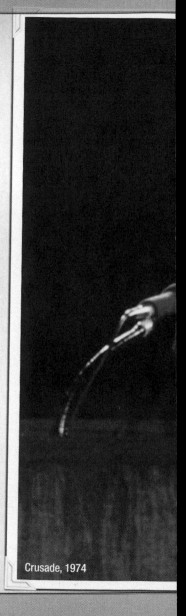

Crusade, 1974

Seek First His Kingdom *and* His Righteousness

I never go to see important people—or anyone else—without having the deep realization that I am—first and foremost—an ambassador of the King of kings and Lord of lords. From the moment I enter the room, I am thinking about how I can get the conversation around to the Gospel. We may discuss a dozen peripheral things first, but I am always thinking of ways I can share Christ and His message of hope with them. I make every effort to be sensitive to their position and their viewpoint, but I rarely leave without attempting to explain the meaning of the Gospel unless God clearly indicates to me that it is not the right time for this person. No one has ever rebuffed me or refused to listen to me.

BILLY GRAHAM, *Just As I Am*

Premier Li Peng,
Beijing, China, 1988

Speaking with students, 1965

Life Principle 5

In Humility Consider Others Better *than* Yourselves

In spite of the widespread impact of his ministry, Billy Graham has never claimed glory for himself, but only for God.

※ ※ ※ ※ ※ ※ ※ ※ ※ ※ ※ ※ ※ ※ ※

Brody Griffith . . . the publisher of the Charlotte paper at that time said, "The evangelist has not permitted his association with presidents and kings to come between his friends in lesser walks of life."

RUSS BUSBY

IN HUMILITY
CONSIDER OTHERS
BETTER *than* YOURSELVES

A well respected man said to me that he had known all of the present day evangelists that had grown up in Billy's era and, "Billy Graham is the only one that God could really use," in his opinion, "because he is the only one that is truly humble enough."

RUSS BUSBY

In Humility
Consider Others
Better *than* Yourselves

One of the nicest editorials ever written about Billy appeared in the *Baptist Standard* many years ago when E. S. James was the editor. This was the feature of his editorial: in spite of all the exposures and the plaudits and the accolades, Billy had maintained the kind of attitude that a Christian minister ought to maintain. It isn't [himself]; it is the Gospel that he proclaims. His humility is there.

James H. Landes

Harlem, 1957

IN HUMILITY CONSIDER OTHERS BETTER *than* YOURSELVES

I remember in New York at the Crusade in 1957 he wanted to change the name from the Billy Graham Evangelistic Association to the American Evangelistic Association or some comparable title. He wanted to remove his name from it. He was out-voted unanimously by everybody on the Team and on the board of directors. I think that was an indication of how the people felt who work with him, also an indication of how he felt. He still is extremely sensitive to the wide publicity and he wishes that it could be avoided.

ROBERT O. FERM

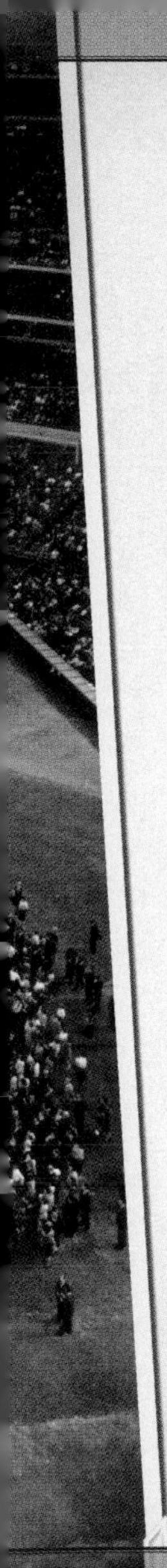

In Humility
Consider Others
Better *than* Yourselves

❧❧❧❧❧❧❧❧❧❧❧❧❧❧❧

As I look back over the years ... I know that my deepest feeling is one of overwhelming gratitude. I cannot take credit for whatever God has chosen to accomplish through us and our ministry; only God deserves the glory, and we can never thank Him enough for the great things He has done.

Billy Graham, *Just As I Am*

A CHEERFUL LOOK BRINGS JOY *to the* HEART

*Although he takes his responsibilities very
seriously, Billy Graham's light-heartedness
pervades his ministry and brings a smile
to the faces of those he touches.*

❧❧❧❧❧❧❧❧❧❧❧❧❧❧❧❧

We were just an average farm family and he
was just an average farm boy, I think, full of
mischief and just having a good time.

CATHERINE G. MCELROY

After we got out of high school, Billy, T.W.
and I went out selling Fuller brushes. . . . We
had a ball that summer. We played more than
we worked. Yet Billy, for some strange reason,
outsold the regional manager of the Fuller
Brush Company of the whole Southeast
Region that summer. He sold more brushes
than anybody in this part of America.

GRADY WILSON

Billy, farmer and salesman

A CHEERFUL
LOOK BRINGS JOY
to the HEART

I had been with other evangelists briefly, but I knew with Mr. Graham, this was something that seemed to be a beginning, that was going to bring good results. . . . I just knew he would be having more and more invitations. People would want to hear him more and more. . . . I felt that way about him when I first met him. He came in the office, tall, open-faced, honest, smiling and laughing. What he said always made such sense, and yet he had a kind of teasing quality.

GEORGE BEVERLY SHEA

George Beverly Shea
and Billy Graham

A CHEERFUL
LOOK BRINGS JOY
to the HEART

Golf gave me not only a way to relax but also, when played with well-known people, a chance to exercise my ministry in a relaxed, informal way. Golf games (and other informal encounters) with the President bonded us more closely at the spiritual level.

BILLY GRAHAM, *Just As I Am*

On the golf course, 1972

President Syngman Rhee,
South Korea, 1951

Life Principle 7

LISTEN *to* HIS VOICE

Billy Graham is a man who listens to the still, small voice of God and obeys it.

I've noticed in my own life . . . Billy's ability to sense people. . . . He's a great student of human nature. He is intuitive and I can remember two or three times when he has almost read my mind and heart.

LEIGHTON FORD

60

Billy in his study, 1968

LISTEN *to*
HIS VOICE

I've been impressed, as have others, that he does not repeat his message. He's always on the look-out for new ways to say it. Of course, he doesn't read but a paragraph or two occasionally. He could repeat the sermon on "The American Home" word for word. It would be marvelous, but he never has. He has to get out new thoughts. He's not an evangelist who has a file full of sermons that he keeps repeating.

GEORGE BEVERLY SHEA

Billy in Peachtree Arcade Building, Atlanta, GA, 1950

LISTEN *to* HIS VOICE

I have noticed a certain characteristic in his preaching that sets it apart from the preaching of anyone else that I've heard.... When he goes into the pulpit to preach ... you can't help but notice a very supernatural power taking hold of him. . . . This is something that is not contrived or deliberate because no one could do it that well.... He can hold the attention of the people out there at a considerable distance who can't really see him well enough to be sure of his physical appearance or anything else. They're just seeing that there is a man up there. But what they are hearing is something quite different. It's the fact that God is working through a man to such a degree that he is communicating a message that God wants him to hear.

ROBERT O. FERM

Seeking the Lord

LISTEN *to*
HIS VOICE

Many people responded to my preaching by confessing faith in Christ and being converted. My teachers and classmates seemed to affirm that this ministry was good and right for me. But did I want to preach for a lifetime? I asked myself that question for the umpteenth time on one of my nighttime walks around the golf course. The inner, irresistible urge would not subside. Finally, one night, I got down on my knees at the edge of one of the greens. Then I prostrated myself on the dewy turf. "O God," I sobbed, "if you want me to serve you, I will." The moonlight, the moss, the breeze, the green, the golf course—all the surroundings stayed the same. No sign in the heavens. No voice from above. But in my spirit I knew I had been called to the ministry. And I knew my answer was yes.

BILLY GRAHAM, *Just As I Am*

Life Principle 8

HE MUST BECOME GREATER; I MUST BECOME LESS

Billy Graham shares John the Baptist's commitment to step aside so that the full measure of God's glory and power can be revealed.

❊❊❊❊❊❊❊❊❊❊❊❊❊❊

After attending the Pittsburgh School of Evangelism, a student said, "I went to Philadelphia to meet a great man [Billy Graham] and I came home with no other desire than to serve the Gospel of a great Savior."

RUSS BUSBY

School of Evangelism, Birmingham, Alabama, 1972

67 />

67

HE MUST BECOME GREATER; I MUST BECOME LESS

I don't think we have any evangelist who is as anointed as Billy is, in his purity of life, and the kind of New Testament simplicity, which is so beautiful. We have men who are very dramatic. We have men who are very gifted. We have men who have much charisma, but we do not have men who have the established clean record of unselfishness of Christian discipleship that match it. We just don't have them.

JAMES H. LANDES

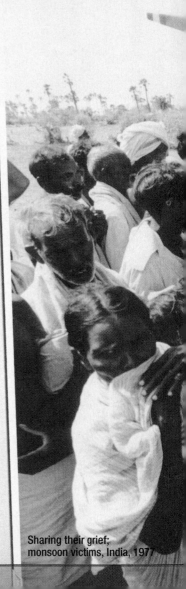

Sharing their grief;
monsoon victims, India, 1977

HE MUST BECOME GREATER; I MUST BECOME LESS

I think my first real understanding of Billy Graham . . . was in the London Crusade in 1954. One night when the largest response came, . . . I asked him, Billy, how do you feel when so many people respond to the invitation? After a moment of thought, he turned and said, "Well, Bob . . . I think I feel about the same way you do. There comes a point where I have to step out. I back away from the microphone and I go into a time of prayer. . . . From then on, I just watch what God is going to do and that's what you'd probably do." . . . He is aware that this is a work of God and he is willing to step out of the limelight at any moment so that the work of God can be carried on.

ROBERT O. FERM

Crusade, 1969

He Must Become Greater; I Must Become Less

Most of all, if anything has been accomplished through my life, it has been solely God's doing, not mine, and He—not I—must get the credit.

BILLY GRAHAM, *Just As I Am*

Portland, Oregon, 1968

Determination

DO NOT SWERVE *to the* RIGHT *or the* LEFT

Billy Graham's commitment to the Lord and to his ministry has never wavered. In spite of the opportunities that have come along, he has remained true to his calling.

⚜ ⚜ ⚜ ⚜ ⚜ ⚜ ⚜ ⚜ ⚜ ⚜ ⚜ ⚜ ⚜ ⚜ ⚜

There were several decisions . . . that he made on his own immediately after his conversion. I can say this: there was never any turning back with Billy. . . . He meant business with the Lord when he was saved. And I believe the Lord has rewarded that.

MORROW COFFEY GRAHAM

Do Not Swerve *to the* Right *or the* Left

Mr. Minder . . . was away that summer and left Billy in charge. Billy went right into Mr. Minder's library and started reading the best books on the Bible. Of course, we had sent him some good books from home on the Bible. He really devoured them and the Word of God. He grew that summer. There was never a letter that came from Billy but what he said something about the Bible and the Lord and how he was studying, how he wanted to grow and how he was praying for growth in his life. Every letter was just full of something like that.

Morrow Coffey Graham

An early sermon

Do Not Swerve *to the* Right *or the* Left

I remember in his junior year, Dr. Edman [the college president] called him in his office and said, "Billy, I see you are booked to be pastor of the Bible Church next year. You can't do that with your heavy schedule. You just can't do it."...And Billy said, "Well, I believe the Lord has called me to do it, Dr. Edman." And they talked and discussed it, pro and con, and Billy still said, "I believe it is the Lord's will. I'm going to make the effort. I may fail, but I'm willing to make the effort." . . . He took [the church position] and got along wonderfully well with it. He was also president of the senior class.

Morrow Coffey Graham

Do Not Swerve *to the* Right *or the* Left

Billy . . . has a heart ministry that reaches the uneducated and he has an intellectual ministry that reaches the educated. And Billy has never slammed anybody . . . or carried on a campaign publicly against his critics. . . . He told me very frankly when I was talking to him one day that he would never answer his critics. He would never try to strike back at them. They had a right to criticize if they wanted to and his job was to preach the Gospel and he was going to stay at his job. . . . And he has never turned back. So I admire him very, very highly on account of the way he has stuck to the work to which God has called him.

Oswald J. Smith

Do Not Swerve *to the* Right *or the* Left

I was in Houston, Texas, when a certain individual wanted Billy to run for President and gave him a check for several millions of dollars to start the program. I'll never forget sitting in Billy's room with members of the Team and how we discussed the different jobs that we would like to have when he was President. Grady wanted to be Secretary of the Interior so he could go hunting, I'll never forget that! George Wilson wanted Postmaster General so he could straighten out the Post Office and I wanted to be Ambassador to Holland. But after all our kibitzing was done, Billy said, "No, the Lord has called me to a different job," and he returned the check.

Robert Van Kampen

Do Not Swerve *to the* Right *or the* Left

During the lunch, Frank made me a proposition: "Billy, MGM has employed an evangelist by the name of Clifford to act in one of their films. But we at Paramount think that your name and ability would be far superior, and I'd like to ask you to consider doing a film with us." I looked him straight in the eye, with the others listening, and told him that God had called me to preach the Gospel and that I would never do anything else as long as I lived. And then I related my own experience with Christ for the benefit of all those at the table.

BILLY GRAHAM, *Just As I Am*

Crusade, 1982

Crusade, 1969

— *Life Principle 10* —
HE DELIGHTS *in* MEN WHO ARE TRUTHFUL

Although he is an international figure, Billy Graham has maintained his genuineness, his integrity and his commitment to being accessible at a personal level.

❈ ❈ ❈ ❈ ❈ ❈ ❈ ❈ ❈ ❈ ❈ ❈ ❈ ❈

I am no hero worshipper and I hate prima donnas . . . but I appreciate Billy personally and if he wasn't real, I couldn't work for him this long. I would not be happy. But I have found him very real and very honest. I don't worship him. I appreciate his ministry . . . and the way in which he presents Christ.

RUSS BUSBY

HE DELIGHTS *in* MEN
WHO ARE TRUTHFUL

Being a small church, we made certain changes that Billy suggested. . . . All of our bulletins and calling cards and our letterhead [said] Village Church and I put on the letterhead, "Rev. William F. Graham, Pastor." Billy would not accept the letterhead and had me do the whole thing over again because he was not going to be called "William" or "Rev. William F. Graham"; it had to be "Billy Graham, Pastor." So I printed the letterheads all over again. . . . I just thought that was proper. That was his name. But Billy said, "No, I want people to call me Billy so that they will feel that they can come to me with any of their problems or needs."

ROBERT VAN KAMPEN

Time for everyone

He Delights *in* Men Who Are Truthful

He has remained true blue. I've met many preachers, evangelists and others. When you get to know them really well, you get disillusioned with some of their operations. But this hasn't been the case with Billy.

Robert Van Kampen

I've come to appreciate this quality: he's not two people. He's his own man. He's the same wherever you meet him.

Robert O. Ferm

Relaxing at home, 1972

He Delights *in* Men
Who Are Truthful

The tendency among some evangelists was to exaggerate their successes or to claim higher attendance numbers than they really had. This likewise discredited evangelism and brought the whole enterprise under suspicion. It often made the press so suspicious of evangelists that they refused to take notice of their work. In Modesto we committed ourselves to integrity in our publicity and our reporting.

BILLY GRAHAM, *Just As I Am*

Crusade, 1950s

JESUS SAID... "I AM THE WAY... THE TRUTH... ...AND THE LIFE"
- JOHN 14

Gulf

Houston, 1965

— Life Principle 11 —

APART FROM ME YOU CAN DO NOTHING

*Billy Graham's awareness
of his dependence on Christ has kept
his ministry rooted in the power of God.*

※※※※※※※※※※※※※※※※

In Lubbock, Texas, at a committee meeting, he said to the committee, "I feel I am a spectator watching what God is doing." He was talking about the Crusade meetings and people coming forward each night.

When Billy stood up to give the closing comments, he said, "All that I have been able to do I owe to Jesus Christ." That to me is the real Billy Graham.

RUSS BUSBY

Jesus said.

In prayer

APART FROM ME YOU CAN DO NOTHING

I remember the first service in Charlotte in 1947: I thought, "This young man has great faith. He's asked the people to come forward. They are singing, and he's got his eyes closed, his hands folded; and he's quiet now. He's not talking like many others." He just quietly waited and prayed as the hymn was being sung, and they came in great numbers.

GEORGE BEVERLY SHEA

SCOTLAND 1991
WITH BILLY GRAHAM

ABERDEEN · PITTODRIE
MAY 30, 31   JUNE 1

APART FROM ME YOU CAN DO NOTHING

As the Crusade gained momentum, I found myself becoming more and more depen-dent on God. I knew that all we had seen happening in Britain was the work of God. If we got in the way or began to take credit for what was happening, God's blessing would be withdrawn. I knew it was also due to the work of the many dedicated people on our Team. I was merely the preacher, the messenger. None of what was happening could have happened apart from God and all the help we had.

BILLY GRAHAM, *Just As I Am*

— *Life Principle* 12 —

WORK TOGETHER
for the TRUTH

*Recognizing the value of teamwork,
Billy Graham has always made sure
that his ministry is about the Team
and the Christian community,
not about him as an individual.*

❊❊❊❊❊❊❊❊❊❊❊❊❊❊

Billy always emphasizes the local church
from the moment he moves into a city [for
a Crusade] until he has gone from the city.
. . . He always includes those leaders so they
know what is going on, and they're not sur-
prised or shocked by the fact that he's there
and enlisting. As a consequence, he moves
with them and they move with him. This
has been true of his emphasis all the way
through. Billy believes in the local church.
He realizes that when he's gone, the local
church is that part of the body of Christ
that must continue to edify and minister
to those who are redeemed by the grace of
our Lord Jesus Christ.

JAMES H. LANDES

Preaching in church, 1980s

Work Together
for the Truth

Something that meant a lot to me was a verse out of 1 Corinthians 3:5, "We are simply God's agents in bringing you to the faith. Each of us performed a task which the Lord allotted to him" (author's paraphrase). And I personally feel this way about the entire Team; each one is doing his task that God has allotted to him. As Billy is the first to admit, it is a team effort.

Russ Busby

Music team, 1967

WORK TOGETHER
for the TRUTH

As I reflect back over half a century, I realize more than ever that this ministry has been a team effort. Without the help of others—our supporters, our prayer partners, our Team and staff, and our board of directors—this ministry would not have been possible.

BILLY GRAHAM, *Just As I Am*

Billy, George Beverly Shea, Cliff Barrows

Preaching in church

Life Principle 13

WHATEVER YOU DO, WORK *at* IT WITH ALL YOUR HEART

Billy Graham has never been afraid of hard work—he has instead embraced it and welcomed it as labor unto the Lord.

I have always thought of him as being a "self-starter." Many students in Bible schools or seminaries, both then and now, will wait until there is a call from a church asking, "Could you please send us someone who can come and teach a Sunday school class?" But Billy never waited for someone to send for him. He made his own openings to go and preach.

ROY GUSTAFSON

Always prepared

WHATEVER YOU DO,
WORK *at* IT WITH ALL
YOUR HEART

As far as his ministry is concerned, . . . Billy
was always prepared. He used to take little
paperback books of Biederwolff's sermons,
I recall, and others of Moody Colportage
books. He would go down on the bank of
the Hillsboro River and put that book on a
cypress stump. He would memorize a paragraph or two and then run up and down
that river bank and preach to the stumps.
. . . He would memorize these sermons and
make them his own.

ROY GUSTAFSON

Whatever You Do, Work *at* It With All Your Heart

Drained as I was, physically, mentally, and emotionally [at the Los Angeles Campaign], I experienced God's unfailing grace in perpetual spiritual renewal. I wanted the Campaign to close, but I was convinced that God wanted it to continue. All my personal reserves were used up; I had to put my entire dependence on the Lord for the messages to preach and the strength to preach them. "[God's] strength is made perfect in weakness," Paul wrote, "for when I am weak, then am I strong" (2 Corinthians 12:9, 10, KJV). It seemed that the weaker my body became, the more powerfully God used my simple words.

BILLY GRAHAM, *Just As I Am*

Southeast Asia, 1975

～ *Life Principle 14* ～

BE . . . NOT GREEDY *for* MONEY, *but* EAGER *to* SERVE

Billy Graham's financial integrity has made him a model of Christian stewardship and has kept his reputation free of critics' reproach.

I'm thrilled to say that I have never seen an organization that so carefully is a steward of God's money in every way, from the office in Minneapolis to every dedicated person. There is not one cent of waste, not a cent. Or of misplaced money. That's excellent, and that's why we support it wholeheartedly.

MARY CROWLEY

Be . . . Not Greedy *for* Money, *but* Eager *to* Serve

In 1949, Cliff Barrows, Billy Graham and I were at Maranatha Bible Conference in Muskegon, Michigan. Billy and Cliff were just becoming well-known. Dr. Henry Savage, the director of the conference, was going to take an offering for Billy's work. However, Billy said: "Please do not give the money to me. Give it to Roy, for his work in the West Indies." The gift was the largest that I had ever received, amounting to over $2,300.00, and made it possible for me to join two others in a Gospel effort in Belize, British Honduras, . . . the first of its kind in that city. A thriving church exists there today.

Roy Gustafson

BE ... NOT
GREEDY *for* MONEY,
but EAGER *to* SERVE

He leans over backwards to avoid criticism. I know this because I was Treasurer and for some years was Chairman of the Executive Committee. I've tried to get Billy to take a larger salary and he absolutely refuses to do it. He said, "I'll take the salary of the pastor of a good-size church because I feel I'm a pastor in that I'm doing a pastor's work and I don't want any special consideration." . . . He feels he is a pastor-at-large and doesn't want to be accused of being in this work for the money. . . . There are two things that Billy has been very careful about. One is money, and the other is that he has never been involved in any kind of scandal of any sort.

ROBERT VAN KAMPEN

Pastor-at-large, 1980s

BE . . . NOT
GREEDY *for* MONEY,
but EAGER *to* SERVE

Like it or not, money is an essential part of any ministry, and safeguards must be put in place to avoid abuses or misunderstandings and to handle all finances with integrity and openness. Most of our financial support comes from the thousands of people who send contributions to us every month. We have no large foundations behind us, and we are dependent on relatively small gifts to meet our expenses every year.

BILLY GRAHAM, *Just As I Am*

With his wife, Ruth,
South Korea, 1973

— Life Principle 15 —

PRAY CONTINUALLY

Prayer has been the underpinning of Billy Graham's ministry and has preceded and surrounded each of his endeavors.

❈❈❈❈❈❈❈❈❈❈❈❈❈❈❈

At a Team meeting one time he made this statement, "Until we believe that men are really lost, we lose the keen sharp edge in our ministry." This is why he is a leader, because he is the first one to humbly go before God in prayer.

RUSS BUSBY

Praying continually

PRAY CONTINUALLY

I will never forget a particular experience that Billy, Logsdon and I had after one of the evening meetings at Maranatha Bible Conference. We three were watching the northern lights. . . . It was time to retire, but someone suggested that we have a time of prayer before separating. Although we were in the middle of a field, we were going to kneel as we prayed. . . . When it was Billy's turn, I opened my eyes for it did not seem that he was praying from a kneeling position. And he wasn't! He, in his good suit, was lying prostrate on the ground, with his face downward. . . . Billy wasn't trying to impress us. . . . Those who know him best will tell you that he is transparent and always has been. That night he was crying out to God for his own life and for his own ministry, that the Lord's hand of blessing would be upon him.

ROY GUSTAFSON

Crusade, ca. 1974

Pray Continually

I once asked Billy Graham why his ministry has been so anointed by God when there are so many other ministries out there that have not had the same kind of impact as his. He said that the Bible tells us to "pray without ceasing" and that the reason why his ministry has been so blessed is that he has actually done it. He prays without ceasing and that makes the difference.

Jerry Jenkins

Pray Continually

How we wrestled in prayer over all our problems. We had prayer meetings at every turn—something I had learned at Florida Bible Institute. What we needed, God provided because of His grace, not because we deserved it.

BILLY GRAHAM, *Just As I Am*

Crusade, 1990s

At Inspirio we love to hear from you —
your stories, your feedback,
and your product ideas.
Please send you comments to us
by way of e-mail at
icares@zondervan.com
or to the address below:

inspirio

Attn: Inspirio Cares
5300 Patterson Avenue SE
Grand Rapids, MI 49530

If you would like further information
about Inspirio and the products
we create, please visit us at:
www.inspiriogifts.com

Thank you and God bless!